Money Matters University for Kids exists to make financial literacy accesible at every age. We do this though four learning modes which allow each student to engage in the material in multiple ways while also facilitating healthy discussion with adults who care for them.

Each of our 24 topics include four modalities including:

Part 1: The Video

Each topic kicks off with a 2-5 minute video from Money Matters University founder, Richard Greco. Through storytelling and teaching, Richard unpacks each lesson's theme in an engaging, age-appropriate, visual learning moment.

Part 2: The Lesson

Each topic is further developed through text-based learning, as we dive into the reading portion which highlights facts and features of that topic, along with examples.

Part 3: The Discussion

We believe that some of the best learning happens when meaningful conversations take place. In our "Let's talk about it!" discussion guide, we encourage students and the caring adults in their life to create time to discuss what financial literacy means to them.

Part 4: The Activity

Lastly, our activity sheets provide students a chance to put what they have learned into practice in a fun and tangible way. With games, decision-making options, and prompts, students get to test out the topic with interactive decision-making.

ISBN: 978-1-968772-00-0

PART ONE: DISCOVERY

PART TWO: KNOWLEDGE

Unpacking Financial Knowledge In 6 Key Lessons:

PART THREE: ACTION

Six Lessons To Equip Kids To Take Healthy Financial Action:

PART FOUR: THRIVING

Six Lessons To Empower Kids To Thrive Financially:

TOPIC #1

WHY MONEY?

https://youtu.be/qAhlsQpRy6c

Watch Here

WHY MONEY?

An introduction to Money Matters University For Kids

WHY DO YOU NEED TO LEARN ABOUT MONEY?

1) You have to deal with money for the rest of your life.

2) Everyone you know needs money and must find a way to earn it.

3) Learning what to do and what not to do with money can make life easier.

4) The earlier you learn about making good choices with your money, the better off you'll be in the future.

WHY MONEY?

LET'S TALK ABOUT IT!

Q1. WHAT DO YOU WANT TO KNOW ABOUT MONEY?
Q2. WHEN IS IT BEST TO LEARN ABOUT HOW TO USE MONEY, NOW OR WHEN YOU'RE OLDER?
Q3. WHAT ARE YOU DOING WELL WITH YOUR MONEY?
Q4. WHAT HELP DO YOU NEED WHEN IT COMES TO UNDERSTANDING HOW TO USE MONEY?

ASK A GROWNUP WHAT THEY WISH THEY WOULD HAVE KNOWN ABOUT MONEY WHEN THEY WERE YOUR AGE.

WHY MONEY?
ACTIVITY SHEET

Draw a picture of yourself enjoying all the things you'd like to have one day with your money.

TOPIC #2

JOB SEARCH

https://youtu.be/41NN3lzbYy0

Watch Here

JOB SEARCH

What do I want to be when I grow up?

HOW PEOPLE CHOOSE THEIR JOBS

1) **Availability**: Who is hiring?

2) **Talent**: What skill do I have?

3) **Pay**: The job provides for my needs.

4) **Interest**: What do I like to do?

5) **Necessity**: I need money now and have to take a job that is available to me.

6) **Location**: Where is the job I want? Where do I want to work?

JOB SEARCH

LET'S TALK ABOUT IT!

Q1. HOW MUCH MONEY DO YOU NEED?
Q2. WOULD YOU MOVE TO ANOTHER CITY FOR A JOB?
Q3. WHAT JOB WOULD MAKE YOU HAPPY?
Q4. DO YOU NEED MORE EDUCATION TO QUALIFY FOR IT?
Q5. IS THERE SOMEONE YOU CAN TALK TO ABOUT THAT JOB?

JOB SEARCH

ACTIVITY SHEET

What do I want to be when I grow up...

When I grow up I want to be a ______________________

because ____

TOPIC #3

NEEDS VS WANTS

https://youtu.be/_jsZtWTc5mE

Watch Here

NEEDS VS. WANTS

In life, you will spend money for things that you need and things that you want. A need is something you must have in order to get by. At this stage, your grown-ups are taking care of your needs for you but as you get older you are responsible for your own needs.

A want is something that would be nice to have. In the diagram below there are two circles. The gray circle represents needs and the green circle represents wants. Where they overlap in the center represents both wants and needs. There are examples below in each category. See if can you add more. Share your own needs and wants.

NEEDS VS. WANTS

LET'S TALK ABOUT IT!

Q1. ARE YOUR NEEDS DIFFERENT THAN A FRIENDS?

Q2. ARE YOUR WANTS ALSO DIFFERENT?

Q3. WHEN COULD A WANT AND NEED TO BE THE SAME THING?

Q4. HOW DO YOU CHOOSE IF SOMETHING IS A WANT OR A NEED?

Q5. WHAT HAPPENS IF YOU PAY FOR A WANT INSTEAD OF A NEED?

NEEDS VS. WANTS
ACTIVITY SHEET

Identifying wants and needs:

At the bottom of the page, you will find pictures of items you may need or want. Draw or cut out these items and put them in the circles. Needs are in the grey circle and wants are in the green circle. Items which are both a need and a want go in the overlap. When you're finished show a grownup and talk to them about where you put the items and see if they would do the same.

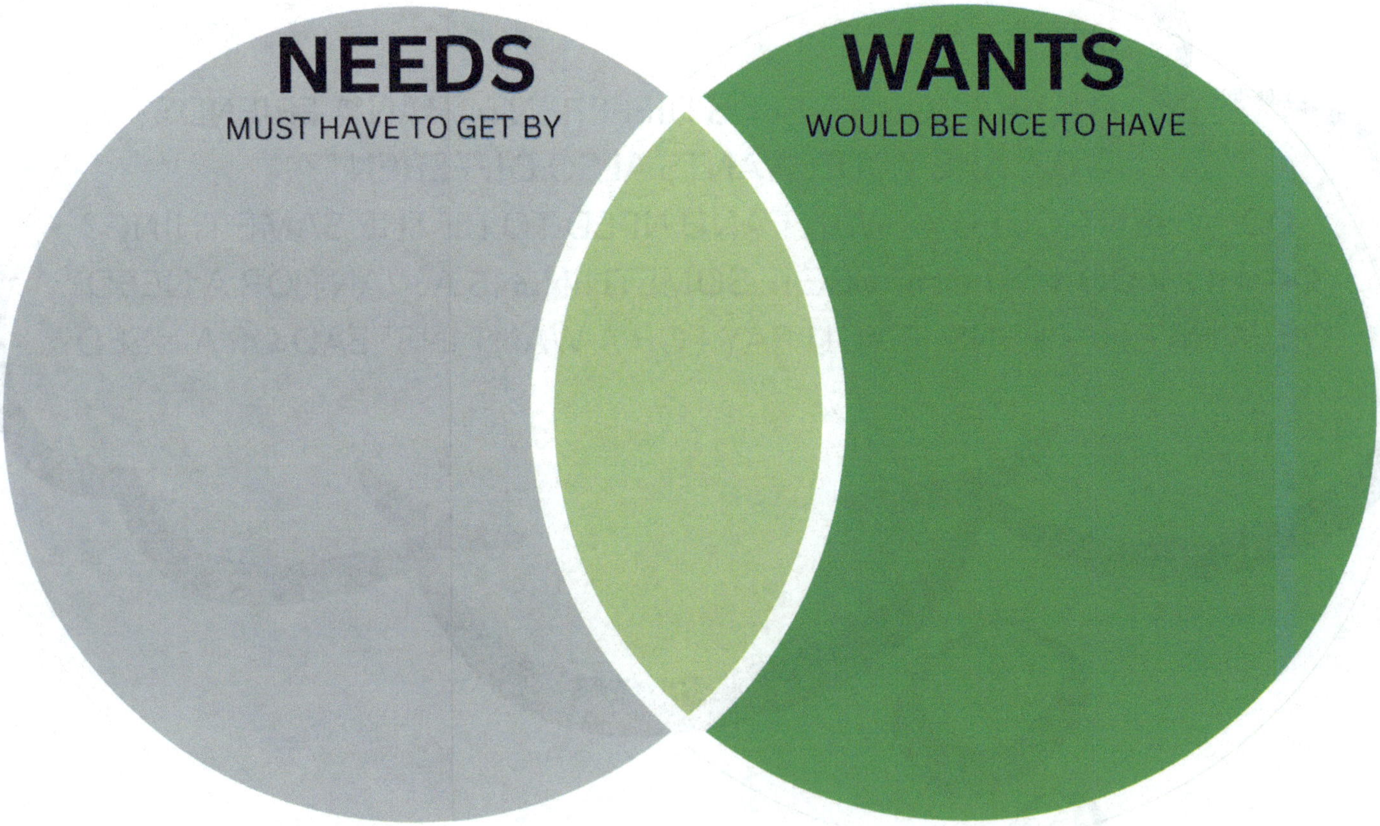

TOPIC #4

BUDGETS

https://youtu.be/K3TME-q6FJ4

Watch Here

WHAT IS A BUDGET?
Why do we need one?

Budget can sound like a scary word, but it doesn't have to be one. Your budget is a plan you create to help you know how much you make, minus how much you spend. When you use the formula: How much money you make minus how much money it takes to pay for your needs and wants, you can answer questions such as:

-Do I have enough money for my needs and wants?

-Do I need to make more money?

-Do I have money left over? And if so, where should I place it in my budget? (Ex. Savings)

How much money you make: your job, chores, etc.

MINUS

How much you pay for your needs and wants

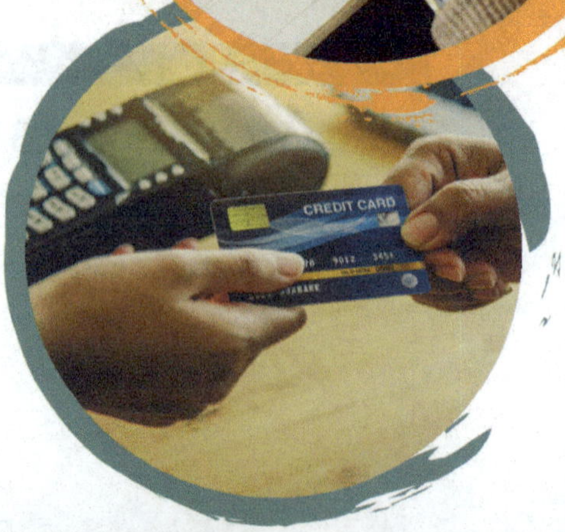

WHAT IS A BUDGET?

LET'S TALK ABOUT IT!

Q1. WHAT IS A BUDGET?
Q2. WHO NEEDS A BUDGET?
Q3. WHEN SHOULD YOU START A BUDGET?
Q4. WHAT COULD HAPPEN IF YOU DO NOT HAVE A BUDGET?

ASK A GROWNUP IF THEY HAVE A BUDGET AND IF THEY CAN HELP YOU CREATE ONE.

WHAT IS A BUDGET?
ACTIVITY SHEET

Now that you know what a budget is, let's practice using one! Below you will find a scale. For this exercise, your monthly budget is $50. You get to decide how to spend your budget. Cut out the items and glue them on the correct side of the scale.

Remember that needs are what you must have and wants are items that would be nice to have. Notice the scale is heavier on the needs side. You will likely need to use most of your budget for your needs.

What did you spend the majority of your budget on?
Did you spend your entire budget?

TOPIC #5

CASH FLOW

https://youtu.be/DC92IEOXJYc

Watch Here

CASH FLOW

Cash flow is money in minus money out.

Examples of money in:

- Chores money
- Yard work
- Lemonade stand

Examples of money going out:

- Rent
- Cell phone bill
- School supplies

Keeping track of your cash flow can:

- Make sure bills are paid on time
- Make you trustworthy to ask to borrow money
- Help you save for a something big you want to buy

Ways to watch your money:

- Create a budget
- Use an envelope system.

CASH FLOW

LET'S TALK ABOUT IT!

Q1. HOW DO YOU GET MONEY?
Q2. WHEN DO YOU GET IT?
Q3. ARE YOU SAVING IT FOR SOMETHING SPECIAL?
Q4. DO YOU KNOW WHAT YOU WILL GET NEXT MONTH?
Q5. WHAT IS IT CALLED WHEN YOU CAN SEE MONEY IN AND MONEY OUT?

ASK A GROWNUP HOW THEY MANAGE THEIR MONEY.

CASH FLOW
ACTIVITY SHEET

YOU'VE RECEIVED $50 FOR YOUR MONTHLY ALLOWANCE. CUT OUT THE MONEY BELOW AND PLACE IT ON THE ENVELOPES TO SHOW HOW YOU WILL SPEND IT. REMEMBER: CASH FLOW IS JUST MONEY IN MINUS MONEY OUT!

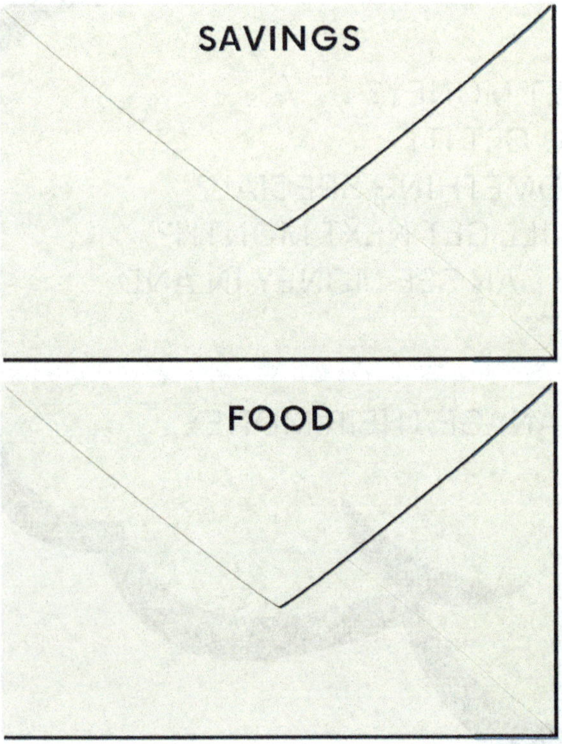

LABEL THIS ONE YOURSELF:

TOPIC #6

NAVIGATING MISTAKES

https://youtu.be/LfCL3h37mRU

Watch Here

NAVIGATING MISTAKES

How do I recover?

WHAT CAN YOU LEARN FROM THE MISTAKES YOU MAKE WITH MONEY?

1) As you learn how to use money, you might make mistakes.

2) Learning from those mistakes helps you grow and make better choices in the future.

3) Ways to avoid mistakes when spending money:
   - Wait a day before buying something special.
   - Ask yourself: Is this thing that I am going to buy a need or a want?
   - Talk to a grown up.

4) Make it a goal to be a life long financial learner in each decision you make.

NAVIGATING MISTAKES

LET'S TALK ABOUT IT!

Q1. HAVE YOU EVER REGRETTED BUYING SOMETHING?

Q2. WHAT DID YOU LEARN FROM THAT?

Q3. WHAT WOULD YOU DO DIFFERENTLY NEXT TIME?

ASK A GROWNUP TO TALK ABOUT A MISTAKE THEY MADE WITH MONEY AND WHAT THEY WOULD DO DIFFERENTLY NEXT TIME.

NAVIGATING MISTAKES
ACTIVITY SHEET

Sometimes we make mistakes with our money. To get back on track, write down a mistake and a solution on each car below. Then place that car on the track. For example: I didn't do my chores and didn't earn an allowance this week. To get back on track, I will ask to do double the chores this week.

MONEY FOR KIDS MATTERS UNIVERSITY

PART TWO: KNOWLEDGE

PART ONE: DISCOVERY

Discovering Financial Habits In Six Key Lessons:

- **Why Money?**
- **Job Search**
- **Needs vs. Wants**
- **Budgets**
- **Cash Flow**
- **Navigating Mistakes**

PART THREE: ACTION

Six Lessons To Equip Kids To Take Healthy Financial Action:

- **Assets & Liabilities**
- **Loans**
- **Taxes**
- **The IRS**
- **The Stock Market**
- **Retirement**

PART FOUR: THRIVING

Six Lessons To Empower Kids To Thrive Financially:

- **Risk Management**
- **Avoiding Scams**
- **Identity Theft**
- **Entrepreneurship**
- **A Business Plan**
- **Financial Success**

TOPIC #7

SELF-DISCIPLINE & CONTENTMENT

https://youtu.be/QE8fAwONWms

Watch Here

SELF-DISCIPLINE & CONTENTMENT

WHAT DOES IT MEAN?

1) Self-discipline is the ability to control how you act and what you do.

2) Contentment is being satisfied with what you have.

3) When it is hard to have self-discipline and contentment it may be difficult to make good decisions.

4) Creating a budget and setting goals are two examples of self-discipline.

5) Achieving the goals often brings contentment.

6) Having self-discipline can lead to a happier life.

SELF-DISCIPLINE & CONTENTMENT

LET'S TALK ABOUT IT!

Q1. WHAT ARE THE WAYS YOU PRACTICE SELF-DISCIPLINE AND CONTENTMENT?
Q2. WHAT ARE THE RESULTS OF NOT PRACTICING IT?
Q3.HOW CAN YOU IMPROVE YOUR SELF-DISCIPLINE?
Q4. DO YOU FEEL CONTENT?
Q5. WHAT ELSE CAN YOU DO?

ASK A GROWNUP TO SHARE ABOUT HOW SELF-DISCIPLINE AND CONTENTMENT HAS HELPED THEM.

SELF-DISCIPLINE & CONTENTMENT
ACTIVITY SHEET

Did you practice self-discipline or contentment?

Read the statements at the bottom of the page and ask yourself, "Is this an act of self-discipline or not?" Put the statement in the correct circle.

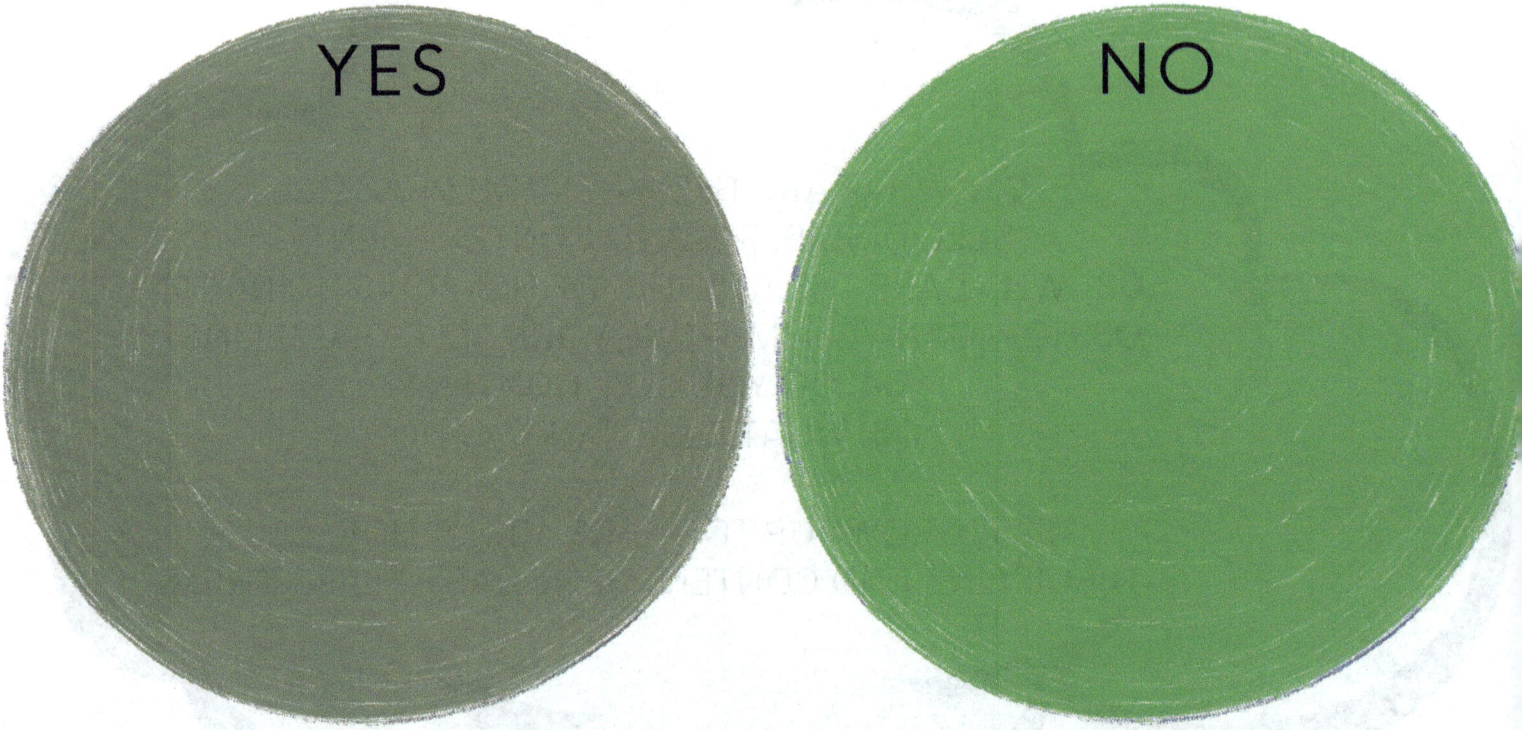

A new phone comes out and I purchase it immediately.

I buy more items than I have on my shopping list.

I donate toys I no longer play with.

My family eats out at restaurants every day.

My family eats at home every day, except Saturday when we visit with friends.

I earn money from chores and give 10% to a local charity.

I go to the store with a grownup and do not ask for anything.

My friend at school has the newest pair of tennis shoes. I borrow money from my parents to buy a pair also. Now I must pay them back.

A new video game is coming out in a month. I do extra chores so I can buy it.

TOPIC #8

SOCIAL RESPONSIBILITY

https://youtu.be/Bf5OEXRf95Q

Watch Here

SOCIAL RESPONSIBILITY

What is my responsibility to my community and the less fortunate?

WHAT IS SOCIAL RESPONSIBILITY?

Supporting our friends and family who are in need.

1) As you earn money, consider those in need as well as meeting your own needs.

2) We can help by giving in three ways:
   - Our time
   - Our talent
   - Our treasure

3) Nothing is ever too small to give.

4) We all need help from time to time. Being part of the solution often brings joy.

5) Helping our friends and family is the right thing to do.

SOCIAL RESPONSIBILITY

LET'S TALK ABOUT IT!

Q1. DO YOU THINK IT IS IMPORTANT TO HELP OUR FRIENDS AND FAMILY?

Q2. WHAT CAN YOU GIVE?

Q3. HOW CAN YOU GIVE OF YOUR TIME OR TALENT?

ASK A GROWN UP ABOUT WAYS THEY HAVE VOLUNTEERED IN THEIR COMMUNITY.

SOCIAL RESPONSIBILITY
ACTIVITY SHEET

How can we GROW our

COMMUNITY?

On the leaves below, write down who you can help. Place them on the tree. Together, we can make a positive difference!

TOPIC #9

FINANCIAL HABITS

https://youtu.be/_m6uF_a77MQ

Watch Here

FINANCIAL HABITS

WHAT POSITIVE HABITS CAN YOU BEGIN TO UTILIZE WITH YOUR MONEY?

1) A financial habit is what you do with your money over and over.

2) People have both good and bad habits.

3) It is best to have good habits. This will usually give you more money for your future.

4) Habits to avoid:
- Spending all of your money as soon as you get it
- Impulse shopping
- Overusing a credit card

5) Good financial habits include:
- Saving a part of your money
- Creating a spending plan (budget)
- Taking care of your needs before your wants

FINANCIAL HABITS

LET'S TALK ABOUT IT!

Q1. WHY ARE
FINANCIAL HABITS IMPORTANT?
Q2. WHAT ARE YOUR GOOD HABITS?
Q3. WHAT HABITS DO YOU NEED TO IMPROVE?
Q4. WHAT WOULD YOU LIKE TO DO TO IMPROVE YOUR HABITS?

ASK A GROWNUP HOW THEY CREATED GOOD FINANCIAL HABITS.

FINANCIAL HABITS
ACTIVITY SHEET

List good habits that will help you to climb to your financial goals.

List bad habits that could make it easy to slip away from your financial goals.

GOOD HABITS

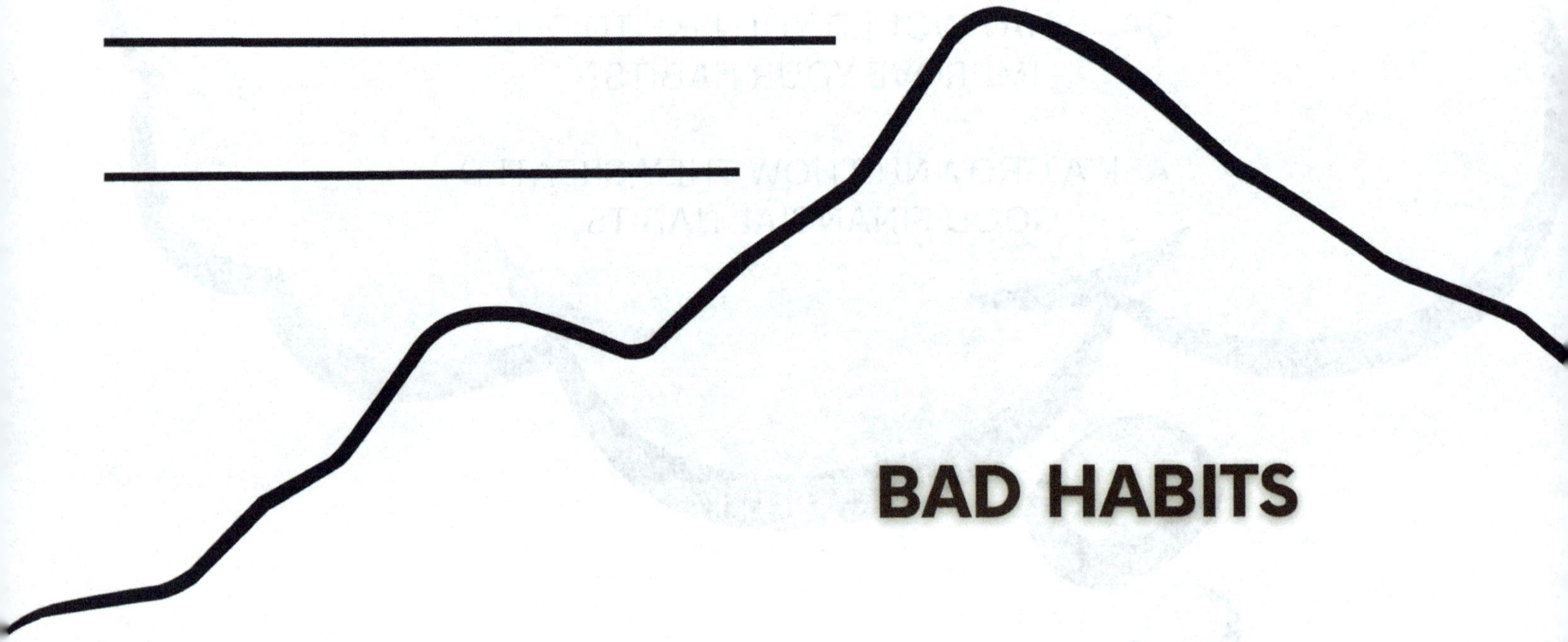

BAD HABITS

TOPIC #10

DEBIT & CREDIT CARDS

https://youtu.be/cYxl8_zxbIY

Watch Here

DEBIT & CREDIT CARDS

What's the difference?

A debit card and a credit card each fit in your wallet. They were created for the convenience of reducing carrying cash. Instead of using cash to buy things, you can use a debit card or credit card. Below are the differences between the two types of cards.

DEBIT CARDS	CREDIT CARDS
Linked to a bank account	You do not need a bank account.
You need to know you have enough money in your bank account to use the card to pay.	Acts like a short-term, interest free loan.
When used, money is immediately taken out of your bank account.	You have 3+ weeks to pay back what you owe.
Risk of fraud is higher	You do not have to pay 100% back right away, but then you pay interest.

DEBIT VS. CREDIT CARDS

LET'S TALK ABOUT IT!

Q1. DO YOU THINK YOU NEED A CREDIT OR DEBIT CARD?

Q2. HOW DO YOU GET A DEBIT OR CREDIT CARD?

Q3. WHAT ARE GOOD HABITS WHEN USING A DEBIT OR CREDIT CARD?

ASK A GROWNUP THEIR THOUGHTS ON BOTH OF THESE CARDS.

DEBIT VS. CREDIT CARDS

ACTIVITY SHEET

There is a list of items at the bottom of the page. These statements are true of either a credit or debit card. Sort them, and place them on either the green debit card or the orange credit card.

DEBIT CARD

CREDIT CARD

Acts like a short-term loan

Money is immediately withdrawn

Can help you stay on budget

Can be saved to use in emergencies

Has better fraud protection

When the money is gone, it's gone

Does not have to be paid back immediately

You may have to pay more, because of interest fees

TOPIC #11

DEBT

https://youtu.be/ydLZT5C-0gs

Watch Here

DEBT

DEBT = THE AMOUNT OF MONEY THAT YOU OWE.

Nature of debt:

- Risky debt is usually bad debt
    - charge on credit card just for fun
    - borrow more money than you can afford to repay
- Investment debt
    - Invest money to start a business
    - Pay for medical bills

Why does anyone get into debt?

- Unexpected hardship
- Foolish spending
- Helping family and friends
- Eating out

Consequences:

- Effects wealth building (good or bad)
- Financial strain
- Decision-making

The best way to manage debt?

- Be aware of your cash flow (know what money is coming in and going out)
- Live below your means
- Reprioritize your needs and wants

DEBT

LET'S TALK ABOUT IT!

Q1. WHO DO YOU KNOW THAT NEVER SEEMS TO HAVE MONEY?

Q2. DO YOU OWN ANYONE MONEY?

Q3. WHAT EXAMPLES OF DEBT ARE VERY RISKY?

Q4. WHAT KIND OF DEBT DO YOU THINK IS OK?

Q5 WHAT CAN YOU DO TO AVOID BAD DEBT IN THE FUTURE?

ASK A GROWNUP HOW THEY HAVE NAVIGATED DEBT.

DEBT
ACTIVITY SHEET

Below is a chart with 3 rows: Debt Free, Minimal Debt, and Maximum Debt. Put each example in the correct rows that represent its impact on debt.

	DEBT FREE	MINIMAL DEBT (NECESSARY DEBT)	MAXIMUM DEBT (UNNECESSARY DEBT)
ELECTRONICS			NEW IPHONE EVERY YEAR
CLOTHES			
FOOD			
HAVING FUN			

CURRENT PHONE	DESIGNER JEANS	EATING OUT EVERY DAY	NEW VIDEO GAMES FOR CHRISTMAS
~~NEW IPHONE EVERY YEAR~~	NEW SCHOOL CLOTHES ON SALE	MAKING MEALS AT HOME	FANCY VACATION
PAYING FOR A USED PHONE OUTRIGHT	KEEPING SHOES THAT STILL FIT	BIRTHDAY DINNER AT YOUR FAVORITE RESTAURANT	GOING TO THE COMMUNITY SWIMMING POOL

TOPIC #12

CREDIT SCORE

https://youtu.be/8YtmLuS8eBs

Watch Here

CREDIT SCORE

1) **Credit score is a number that represents a perceived ability to repay a debt based on your financial history.**

2) **Who has a credit score?**
- Anyone who borrows money or has a credit card gets a credit score
- Credit can be granted by banks, retail stores, credit unions, and other financial funders
- Credit scores range from 300-850

3) **High credit scores grants you the chance to:**
- Get a better interest rates on borrowed money
- Have a positive financial reputation
- Get more financial opportunities

4) **Low credit scores lead to:**
- Less options to borrow money
- High interest rates
- Fewer opportunities

5) **What affects your credit score?**
- Late payments, payment history, identity theft, applying for new credit, bankruptcy, high credit card balances, co-signing a loan, credit inquiries, and many more.

CREDIT SCORE

LET'S TALK ABOUT IT!

Q1. WHAT DO YOU THINK AFFECTS YOUR CREDIT SCORE?
Q2. WHAT IS A GOOD CREDIT SCORE?
Q3.HOW CAN YOU GET A GOOD CREDIT SCORE?

ASK A GROWNUP ABOUT THEIR CREDIT SCORE. ASK THEM TO SHARE WHAT THEY THINK YOU SHOULD KNOW.

CREDIT SCORE
ACTIVITY SHEET

Ways to increase your credit score:

Ways to decrease your credit score:

Make consistent payments on a loan

Going over a credit limit (Spending too much)

Having too many credit cards

Keep your balance on your credit card low

Missing a credit card payment

Applying for a credit card

Make credit card payments early

Paying your bills on time

Closing credit cards

MONEY FOR KIDS MATTERS UNIVERSITY

PART THREE: ACTION

PART ONE: DISCOVERY

Discovering Financial Habits In Six Key Lessons:

PART TWO: KNOWLEDGE

Unpacking Financial Knowledge In Six Key Lessons:

PART FOUR: THRIVING

Six Lessons To Empower Kids To Thrive Financially:

TOPIC #13

ASSETS & LIABILITIES

https://youtu.be/SRBW0_wSv8I

Watch Here

ASSETS & LIABILITIES

Asset: Something you own.
Liability: Something you owe.

Examples of assets:

- Money
- Sports equipment
- Gaming devices
- Cell phone
- Jewelry
- Cameras

Examples of liabilities:

- IOU's
- Loans
- Promise to pay back.

Having more assets than liabilities means you have positive financial worth. This is called your "net worth." Below is how calculate your net worth.

Assets minus liabilities

equals net worth

ASSETS & LIABILITIES

LET'S TALK ABOUT IT!

Q1. WHAT DO YOU HAVE THAT IS VALUABLE TO YOU?
Q2. WHAT WOULD YOU LIKE TO HAVE IN THE NEXT SIX MONTHS?
Q3. DO YOU HAVE ANY DEBT OR OWE ANYONE SOMETHING?

ASK A GROWNUP HOW THEY BUILT THEIR NET WORTH.

ASSETS & LIABILITIES
ACTIVITY SHEET

How to find your net worth. It is all about assets minus liabilities.

Each item below represents an asset or a liability. Determine which is which and then take the sum of your assets and the sum of your liabilities to calculate net worth.

Phone:
$600

Loan:
$300

Bicycle:
$400

Car Repairs:
$1,200

Camera:
$900

Doctor's Bill:
$200

My Assets:

____

____

____

Sum $______________ ***minus***

My Liabilities:

____

____

____

Sum $______________ ***equals***

My Net Worth:

$______________

TOPIC #14

LOANS

https://youtu.be/hTUxyxi2Jko

Watch Here

LOANS

A loan is an agreement to borrow money and pay it back with interest over a certain period of time.

There are common reasons to borrow money:

- Education (Student loans)
- Transportation (Car loans)
- Living (Mortgage)
- Career (Investing in a business)

Here is the typical process to get a loan:

- Go to your bank to meet with a lender
- Apply for a loan by providing your financial information

Consequences of applying for a loan:

- The bank will check your credit score to determine how much you qualify for.
- This check will increase or decrease your credit worthiness.

A loan is a debt that has interest.

- The longer you take to pay back a debt, the more you will owe on the original amount. This is called interest. You pay what you borrowed, plus a fee.

LOANS

LET'S TALK ABOUT IT!

Q1. WHAT IS THE MAIN BENEFIT OF A LOAN?
Q2. WHAT ARE COMMON REASONS FOR A LOAN?
Q3. WHY MIGHT YOU BE DENIED A LOAN?

ASK A GROWNUP IF THEY HAVE ANY ADVICE ON TAKING OUT LOANS.

LOANS
ACTIVITY SHEET

Below you will see pictures of needs many people have or choose to have. Often, people take out loans to be able to meet these needs. Draw a line to match each description to each picture.

CAREER:
BUSINESS LOAN

TRANSPORTATION:
CAR LOAN

EDUCATION:
STUDENT LOAN

HEALTH:
MEDICAL LOANS

LIVING:
MORTGAGE

TOPIC #15

TAXES

https://youtu.be/hqL5MoXox2U

Watch Here

TAXES

What should you know about taxes?

What is a tax?
A government fee to support services that pay for needs in our country and community. Although many people may not want to pay taxes, it is the law and we are required to do so.

Who pays taxes and what are they for?

- Homeowners (real estate/property tax)
- Employees (income tax)
- Employers (business tax)
- Consumers (sales tax)

What services do taxes pay for?

- Public schools
- Public libraries
- Infrastructure (roads, lights, bridges)
- Public playgrounds and recreation
- Public beaches

TAXES

LET'S TALK ABOUT IT!

Q1. HOW DO YOU THINK TAXES IMPROVE YOUR NEIGHBORHOOD?

Q2. WHAT TYPES OF TAXES EXIST?

Q3. WHEN ARE YOU REQUIRED TO PAY INCOME TAXES?

ASK A GROWNUP HOW THEY MANAGE THEIR TAXES.

TAXES
ACTIVITY SHEET

For every dollar you earn at work, below is the approximate breakdown of how much you will take home and how much will go towards state, local, and federal taxes.

67%- TAKE HOME PAY | **33%-TAXES**

33% { 5%-state/local
20%-federal
8%- social security, medicare

Place a check mark by the photos below that represent some of the services you enjoy that taxes pay for.

TOPIC #16

THE IRS

https://youtu.be/iPj5dyzuNvY

Watch Here

THE IRS

The IRS is a government agency responsible for collecting taxes.

- The IRS interprets tax law and monitors people and businesses to assure everyone pays their fair share of taxes.
- They conduct audits as they see fit to validate that taxes are properly paid.

Some fun facts about the IRS:

- The IRS started during the Civil War.
- They monitored the 1920 prohibition.
- They took down Al Capone.
- There are over 70,000 pages in the IRS code.
- They currently employ over 100,000 people.
- In a recent year, they collected $4.7 trillion in revenue.
- They process 271 million tax returns.

All money earned from work is taxed. Whoever hires you tells the IRS how much money you receive. Every year, you pay taxes based on that amount.

The IRS publishes forms and instructions to help us be able to file correctly.

THE IRS

LET'S TALK ABOUT IT!

Q1. HAVE YOU HEARD OF THE THE INTERNAL REVENUE SERVICE (THE IRS) BEFORE TODAY?

Q2. IF SO, WHAT HAVE YOU HEARD?

Q3. HOW DOES THE IRS BENEFIT OUR COUNTRY?

ASK A GROWNUP WHAT THEY KNOW ABOUT THE IRS.

THE IRS

ACTIVITY SHEET

When you begin working, do you want to work for someone or have your own business? This determines what forms need to be completed, starting with either the W-4 or W-9.

I AM AN EMPLOYEE

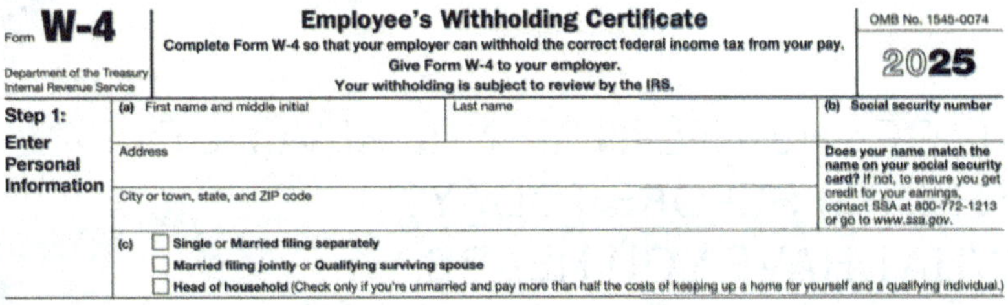
Form W-4 Employee's Withholding Certificate 2025
Complete Form W-4 so that your employer can withhold the correct federal income tax from your pay.
Give Form W-4 to your employer.
Your withholding is subject to review by the IRS.

I OWN MY OWN BUSINESS

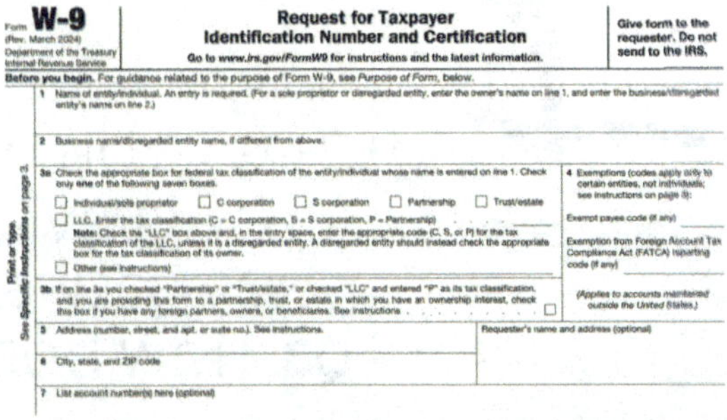
Form W-9 Request for Taxpayer Identification Number and Certification

Every employer will report your income to the IRS, with these forms.

I AM AN EMPLOYEE

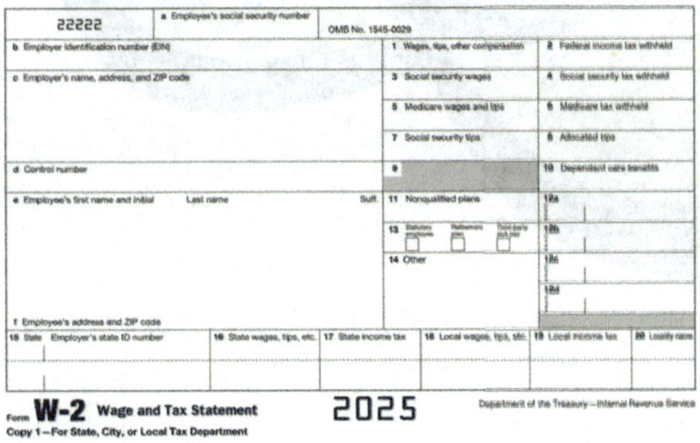
Form W-2 Wage and Tax Statement 2025

I OWN MY OWN BUSINESS

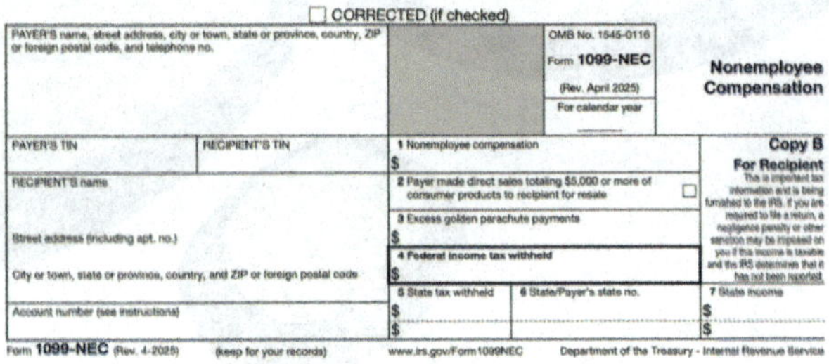
Form 1099-NEC Nonemployee Compensation

Whether you are an employee or own your own business, all income must be filed on a 1040 each year.

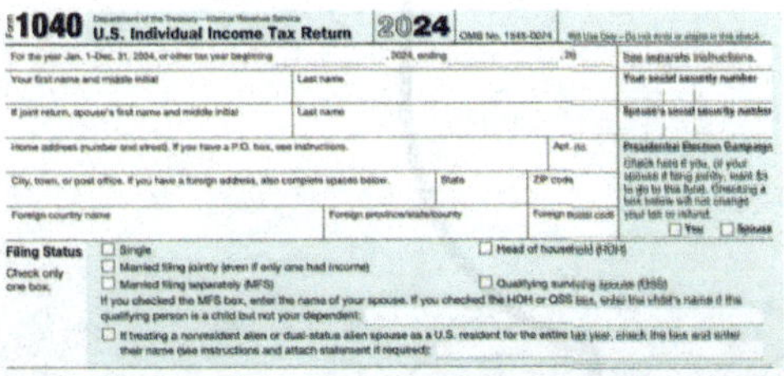
1040 U.S. Individual Income Tax Return 2024

For this exercise: Ask a grownup to go to IRS.gov, search for these forms, print them, and complete them with you to practice filling one section out.

TOPIC #17

THE STOCK MARKET

https://youtu.be/HKocwnnDIkU

Watch Here

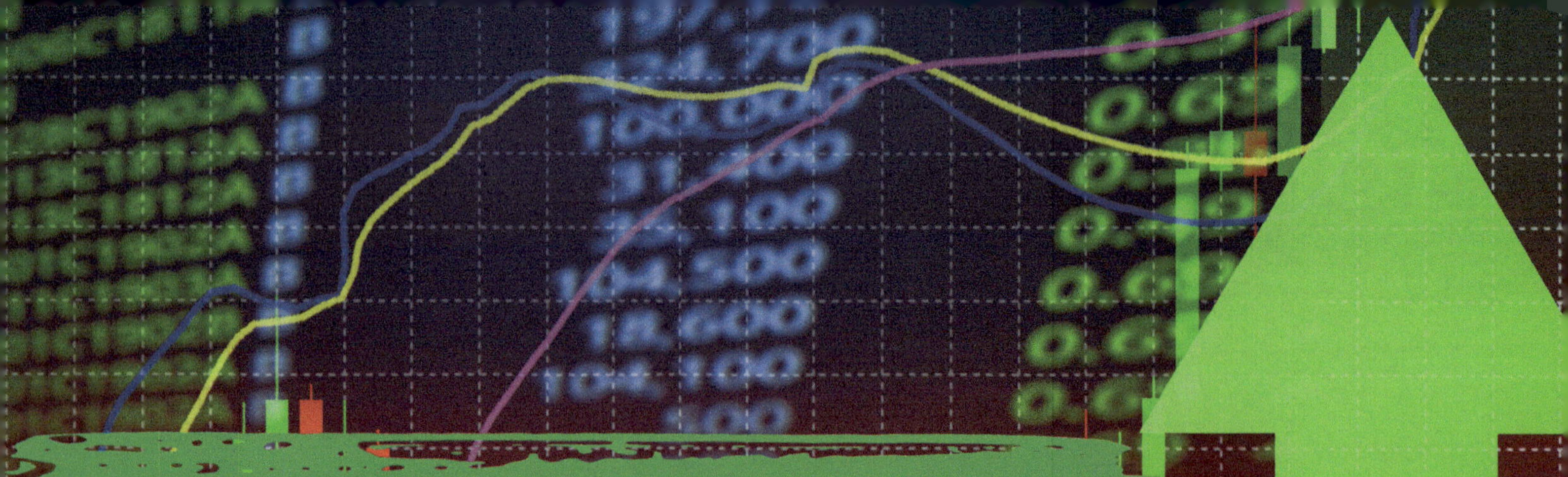

THE STOCK MARKET

What do you need to know about the stock market?

What is the stock market?

The stock market is comprised of various organizations that monitor the sale of stock for public companies. The are called exchanges and include:

- Dow Jones
- OTC
- NYSE
- NASDAQ
- S&P500

Why do people invest?

- You have extra money and want to make more money by investing.
- You believe in the mission of a specific company and want to own part of it.

How do you invest in stocks?

- You decide which stock you want.
- You or a financial advisor purchase the stock from an exchange.

THE STOCK MARKET

LET'S TALK ABOUT IT!

Q1. WHY DO COMPANIES ISSUE STOCK?

Q2. WHAT ARE THE BENEFITS OF THE STOCK MARKET?

Q3. HOW COULD THE STOCK MARKET BE RISKY?

Q4. WHY DO SOME PEOPLE HIRE A FINANCIAL ADVISOR TO INVEST MONEY FOR THEM?

ASK A GROWNUP IF THEY INVEST IN THE STOCK MARKET.

THE STOCK MARKET
ACTIVITY SHEET

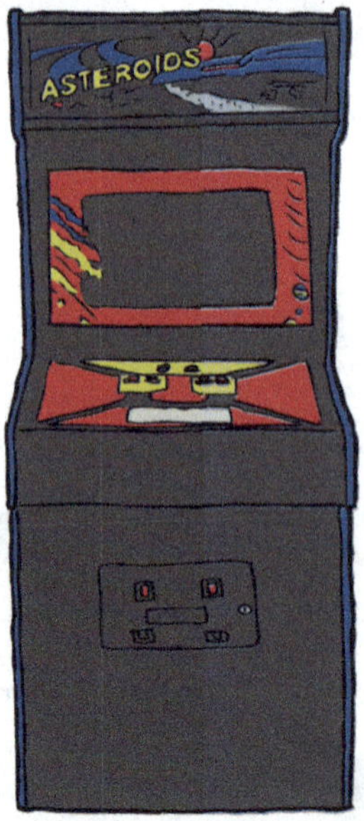

Let's imagine you are at an arcade. There are prizes you want to win. But you only have so many tokens. How can you get the most amount of prizes with how many coins you have?

Below are the prizes you could get. Decide what you want.

Step 1: Circle the prizes below that you would like to earn. For right now, don't think about how many coins you have to spend.

Controller
300 tickets

Candy
5 tickets per piece

Stuffed Animal
100 tickets

Drum
125 tickets

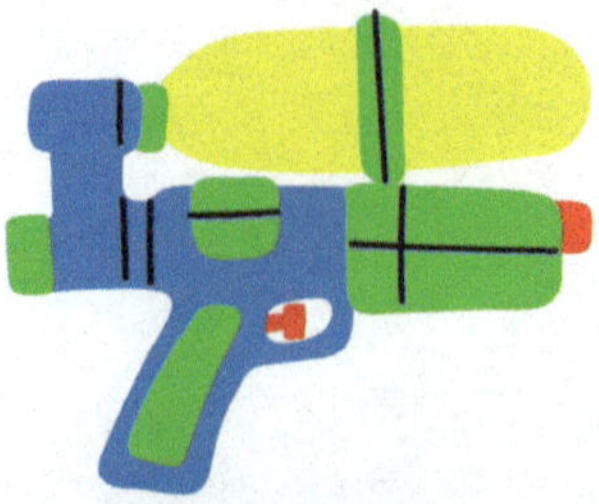

Water Gun
175 tickets

Beach Ball
35 ticketss

THE STOCK MARKET
ACTIVITY SHEET

Step 2: Calculate the amount of coins you need to earn the amount of tickets you need for that prize. For this activity, imagine you have 25 coins to play 3 arcade games. Each game costs a different amount and may give fewer or more tickets.

Game 1
Coins to play: 2
Tickets possible: 5-15

Game 2
Coins to play:3
Tickets possible: 10-30

Game 3
Coins to play:4
Tickets possible: 25-45

Step 3: Write down how many coins you will spend on each game :

Game One:

Game Two:

Game Three:

When you look at how you chose to spend your coins, how likely are you to win the prizes you selected in step 1?

TOPIC #18

RETIREMENT

https://youtu.be/wsdVDAXADTo

Watch Here

RETIREMENT

What do you need to know about retirement now?

What is retirement?

Retirement is decision to stop working. Hopefully, you have enough money saved to pay for your needs.

When is the right time to retire?

- I have had my finances evaluated and know I have enough money to keep my lifestyle without working anymore
- I am ready to stop working
- It is better for my heath if I stop working.

RETIREMENT AWARENESS

Pros:

- You track current finances
- You plan to move into a new stage of life one day
- You can make more flexible decisions for your career
- You have financial security

Cons:

- Later in life, you may have to sell investments to pay for retirement.
- You may have to focus more on needs than wants.

RETIREMENT

LET'S TALK ABOUT IT!

Q1. WHY IS IT IMPORTANT TO TALK ABOUT RETIREMENT BEFORE YOU START WORKING?
Q2. WHAT HAVE YOU HEARD ABOUT RETIREMENT?
Q3. DO YOU THINK EVERYONE HAS TO RETIRE SOMEDAY?

ASK A GROWNUP TO MAKE A LIST OF ALL THE THINGS THEY'D LIKE TO DO IN RETIREMENT.

RETIREMENT
ACTIVITY SHEET

Saving for retirement can feel like a maze. The goal of this activity is to move from "start" to "retirment." Name the roadblocks which prevent you from making it to retirement.

What roadblocks do you imagine prevent someone from being able to retire when they want?

Roadblock #1 ______________________________

Roadblock #2 ______________________________

Roadblock #3 ______________________________

Roadblock #4 ______________________________

PART FOUR: THRIVING

PART ONE: DISCOVERY

Discovering Financial Habits In Six Key Lessons:

PART TWO: KNOWLEDGE

Unpacking Financial Knowledge In Six Key Lessons:

PART THREE: ACTION

Six Lessons To Equip Kids To Take Healthy Financial Action:

TOPIC #19

RISK MANAGEMENT

https://youtu.be/2l36t17BlXg

Watch Here

RISK MANAGEMENT

What is risk and how can you stay safe?

RISK MANAGEMENT IS A WAY OF TAKING ACTION TO LIMIT BAD THINGS FROM HAPPENING.

The goal is not to live afraid. Risk management is less about dwelling on the bad things that could happen, and more about learning what we can do to stay healthy and safe.

Ways people manage risk:

- By eating healthy, exercising, and taking care of their bodies
- By having an insurance plan
- By wearing protective gloves, hats, helmets, gear, sunscreen, and more.
- By using caution when driving.

Just like putting on a seat belt to stay safe in the car, or bringing an umbrella to stay dry, risk management is about doing our part to limit harm.

RISK MANAGMENT

LET'S TALK ABOUT IT!

Q1. WHAT KIND OF RISKS DO YOU TAKE?
Q2. WHAT DO YOU DO TO PROTECT YOURSELF?
Q3. WHAT RISKS DO YOU NOT EVEN THINK ABOUT?
Q4. HAVE YOU EVER USED PROTECTIVE EQUIPMENT FOR A SPORTING EVENT OR GAME?

ASK A GROWNUP HOW THEY PROTECT THEMSELVES AND THE FAMLY.

RISK MANAGMENT
ACTIVITY SHEET

For the following items, write down the risk and what action you can take to limit that risk.

What is the risk? **How can I limit that risk?**

TOPIC #20

AVOIDING SCAMS

https://youtu.be/-1-V_gqg1Ms

Watch Here

AVOIDING SCAMS

A scam is when someone tricks you to steal your money.

How can you protect yourself and your money?

1) Only talk to someone you know and trust.

2) Never give anyone your personal or financial information.

3) Look at your bank account daily.

4) Never click on a link, email, or ad from anyone you don't know.

5) Ask a trusted adult when using the internet when buying anything.

6) Do not share your password with anyone.

AVOIDING SCAMS

LET'S TALK ABOUT IT!

Q1. WHAT SHOULD YOU DO IF YOU GET AN EMAIL SAYING YOU WON A NEW PHONE?

Q2. HOW CAN YOU PROTECT YOURSELF FROM A SCAM?

Q3. WHAT SHOULD YOU DO IF SOMEONE ASKS FOR YOUR ADDRESS TO DELIVER A PRIZE?

TALK TO A GROWNUP ABOUT WAYS TO STAY SAFE.

AVOIDING SCAMS
ACTIVITY SHEET

Scams happen in many ways. But we get to choose our response and how to stay safe. For each scam listed below, choose your response from the five actions at the bottom of this page. There can be more than one response. Discuss your responses with a grownup. Get their input. If you can think of another scam, add it and write a response for it as well.

SCAM	RESPONSE
You've won a contest you don't remember entering	
You're asked for your address to get a prize	
You're asked to send a smaller amount of money to receive a larger amount	
You're asked for bank information or a Social Security number	
You're told you owe a debt and they will collect it for you	
Social media asks for "get to know you" information to retrieve security question answers	
You receive a friend request from someone you do not and could not know	

1) Talk to a grownup

2) Do not give personal info

3) Hang up

4) Do not open the link

5) Do not participate

TOPIC #21

IDENTITY THEFT

https://youtu.be/UdxSP05jzvl

Watch Here

IDENTITY THEFT

Identity theft is when another person represents themselves as you - without your knowledge - in order to take over financial control.

1) Common ways identity theft can occur:

- Sharing private financial information in a public location
- Using the internet without appropriate protection and security
- Discarding physical documents with confidential information without shredding

2) Results of identity theft:

- Loss of money and/or possessions
- Damaged credit score
- Time required to solve the theft

3) Steps to take if you suspect you've been a victim of identity theft

- Tell a grownup immediately
- Take an inventory of your assets (ex. credit card, debit card, driver's license)
- Change passwords to all online accounts
- Contact your bank

4) Ways you can protect yourself:

- Never give out financial information to someone you do not know.
- Keep track of your belongings (credit cards, etc.)
- Change your passwords regularly

IDENTITY THEFT

LET'S TALK ABOUT IT!

Q1. WHY IS IS IMPORTANT FOR YOU TO KNOW ABOUT IDENTITY THEFT?

Q2. HOW CAN YOU MINIMIZE IDENTITY THEFT AND PROTECT YOUR ASSETS?

Q3. WHO DO YOU THINK IS MOST AT RISK FOR IDENTITY THEFT?

ASK YOUR GROWNUP WHAT THEY KNOW ABOUT IDENTITY THEFT.

IDENTITY THEFT
ACTIVITY SHEET

Taking care of items that contain your personal information is the best thing you can do to protect yourself from identity theft. These items can include your full name, phone number, address, passwords, Social Security number, driver's license, credit card, debit card, as well as other items.

How do you know what is safe to share with others and is private information? Place each of the following items in the two categories below and then talk about your answers with a grownup.

OK TO TALK ABOUT

KEEP PRIVATE

Your favorite color

Your phone number

Your gaming password

Your address

Your favorite TV show

Your bank info

Your pet's name

Your credit card number

Your dream job

TOPIC #22

ENTREPRENEURSHIP

https://youtu.be/ZqGjfqPXRw4

Watch Here

ENTREPRENEURSHIP

Entrepreneurship means starting a business. Anyone can be an entrepreneur.

1) What are the traits of an entrepreneur?

- A person who seeks to work for themselves
- A person with drive and commitment

2) What do you need to start a business?

- An idea
- A clear picture of who would want it
- A business plan
- A name for your business.
- Guidance from a professional on how to setup your business (attorney, accountant, mentor, etc.)

3) What are the positives about being an entrepreneur?

- Being your own boss
- Creating your own rules
- Ability to control the business
- Freedom to make decisions

4) What challenges do entrepreneurs face?

- Being responsible whether you succeed or not
- Balancing work and free time
- Remaining focused
- Keeping customers satisfied

ENTREPRENEURSHIP

LET'S TALK ABOUT IT!

Q1. IF YOU WERE TO START YOUR OWN BUSINESS, WHAT WOULD YOU DO?

Q2. DO YOU PREFER WORKING BY YOURSELF OR WITH SOMEONE?

Q3. WHO DO YOU TALK TO WHEN YOU NEED HELP?

ASK A GROWNUP WITH A BUSINESS WHAT THEY LIKE AND DISLIKE ABOUT BEING THEIR OWN BOSS.

ENTREPRENEURSHIP
ACTIVITY SHEET

Ready to start your own business? Congrats! Let's decide what you need to get started.

What are you going to name your company?

How much will you charge for the items?

What items will you sell?

Will you hire anyone?

What are your goals?

Who do you know that can help you?

TOPIC #23

A BUSINESS PLAN

https://youtu.be/luzdmNV5ke8

Watch Here

A BUSINESS PLAN

A business plan is a written document outlining how you intend to run your business.

There are three creations to starting something new

- An idea in the brain
- A plan on paper
- A physical model

Starter steps for a business plan include:

- Define the vision as if it has already happened
- Sketch or make a model of the final product
- Create a supply list
- Purchase supplies (Make sure to have a budget.)
- Create Item
- Identify your customers

Questions to ask:

- Why is this product or service needed?
- How much would your customers pay?
- Can you make this yourself or do you need help to create it?

A BUSINESS PLAN

LET'S TALK ABOUT IT!

Q1. WHAT PRODUCT DO YOU WANT TO CREATE?

Q2. WHAT STEPS COULD YOU TAKE TO START A BUSINESS?

Q3. CONSIDER WHAT NEEDS TO BE IN YOUR BUSINESS PLAN.

ASK A GROWNUP IF THEY HAVE OR HAD A BUSINESS IDEA THAT THEY WOULD LIKE TO SHARE.

A BUSINESS PLAN
ACTIVITY SHEET

Choose a business you would like to start. Follow the steps below to create your own business plan.

Draw a picture of your idea.

Create a list of your potential customers.

____

____

____

____

____

____

____

How much do your supplies cost?

____

How much will you sell your product for?

____

TOPIC #24

FINANCIAL SUCCESS

https://youtu.be/hYKepj5Iaso

Watch Here

FINANCIAL SUCCESS

What does financial success look like to you? To experience true financial success, you must have all of your needs met. This allows you to also take care of your wants. Everyone is different. Think about what you value and what is important to you. Below is a list of examples of personal and financial success.

PERSONAL SUCCESS	FINANCIAL SUCCESS
You enjoy your job and have a fulfilling career.	You are self-employed and in control over your day.
You have a healthy relationship with family.	You own a house without a mortgage.
You received a full education in order to meet your goals.	You have enough money in the bank for your lifestyle.
You have healthy children who are thriving.	You have the ability to take vacations.
You have financial freedom: All of your needs are met.	You have enough money to purchase your wants.

FINANCIAL SUCCESS

LET'S TALK ABOUT IT!

Q1. WHAT IS YOUR MEASUREMENT OF DO YOU KNOW IF YOU ARE FINANCIAL SUCCESS?

Q2. WHAT ACTIONS HAVE YOU TAKEN TO IMPROVE YOUR FINANCIAL SUCCESS?

Q3. WHAT CHALLENGES DO YOU FACE?

ASK A GROWN UP HOW THEY DEFINE FINANCIAL SUCCESS FOR THEMSELVES.

FINANCIAL SUCCESS
ACTIVITY SHEET

What does personal and financial success look like to you? Fill out the sheet below and talk with a grownup about your goals.

PERSONAL SUCCESS	FINANCIAL SUCCESS

Made in United States
North Haven, CT
04 November 2026

21760193R00063